This book belongs to

_____

This book is dedicated to my children - Mikey, Kobe, and Jojo.

Paperback ISBN: 978-1-63731-462-3
Hardcover ISBN: 978-1-63731-464-7
eBook ISBN: 978-1-63731-463-0

Printed and bound in the USA.
NinjaLifeHacks.tv

Ninja Life Hacks™

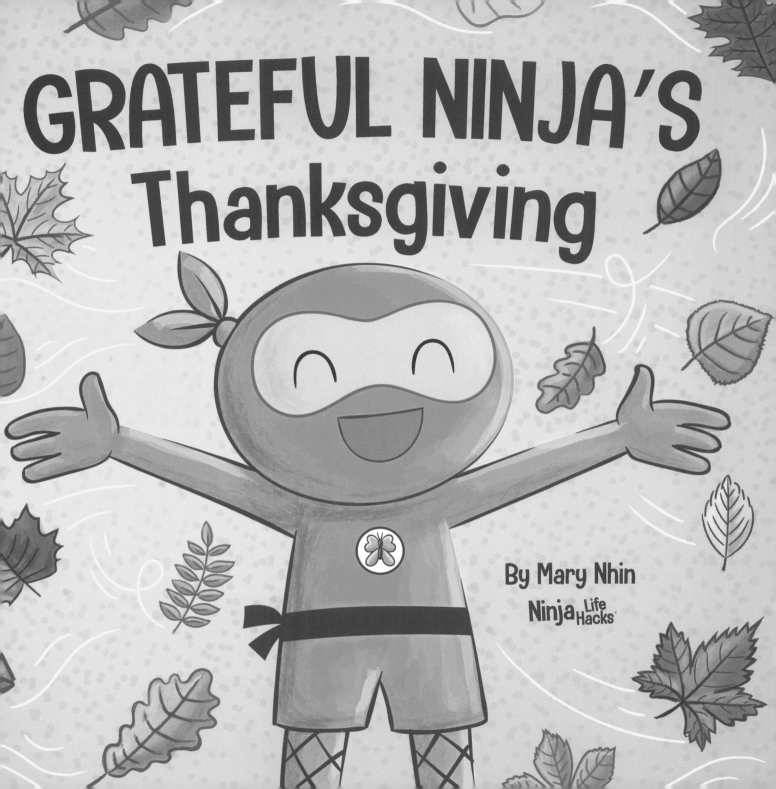

GRATEFUL NINJA'S
Thanksgiving

By Mary Nhin

Ninja Life Hacks

And then, at school, it's activity time,
This is going to be great.
'Today, it's all about hands,' Teacher says,
'Whose hands do you appreciate?'

Then there are grandparents' hands as well,
They may be wrinkly and old.
But these hands have seen so many things,
Each wrinkle's a story to be told.

$$1 + 1 = 2$$
$$2 + 2 = 4$$
$$3 + 3 = 6$$
$$4 + 4 = 8$$
$$5 + 5 = 10$$

$$2 / 1 = 2$$
$$4 / 2 = 2$$

'They taught me how to count and spell,
And how to pass a test.
These hands belong to my teacher,
Who I think is the **BEST!**'

Thanks for being a loyal ninja reader. I hope you enjoyed this story. I love to hear from my readers. Please email me your feedback, story, and product ideas at growgritpress@gmail.com

Use code THANKS to download your free Grateful Ninja's Gratitude Prompts at ninjalifehacks.tv

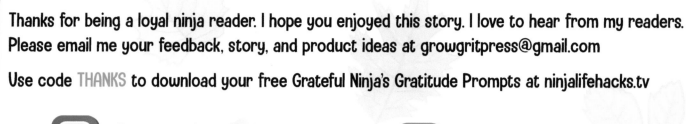 @marynhin   @GrowGrit
#NinjaLifeHacks

Mary Nhin   Ninja Life Hacks

Ninja Life Hacks

@ninjalifehacks.tv